Contents

Welcome to a village

When you visit an historic site, use all your senses to get as much from your visit as possible. Smell the sweet aroma of bread baking in a hot oven. Touch the coarse wool that is being spun into yarn. Taste some old-fashioned candy at the general store. Listen to the sound of the hammer hitting red-hot iron in the blacksmith shop. Imagine that you are part of this old way of life, and remember to ask plenty of questions.

Have you ever visited a home or community from the past? These homes and villages are called **historic** because they teach us about a special time long ago. They can be found in many places. You may live close to one. If not, you can "visit" an historic village by reading this book. Although the pictures come from several villages that existed at different times in history, they show the important things that many early settlements had in common.

An historic village is a community. A community can be two things. It is a group of people who live in one area, but it is also the place where

HISTORIC
COMMUNITIES

Visiting a Village

Bobbie Kalman

SCHOLASTIC INC.
New York Toronto London Auckland Sydney

HISTORIC
COMMUNITIES

Created by Bobbie Kalman

For Andrea

Editors
Christine Arthurs
Marni Hoogeveen

Design
Heather Delfino

Pasteup
Adriana Longo

Visiting a Village is part of the Historic Communities series.

Copyright © 1990 by Crabtree Publishing Company.
All rights reserved. Published by Scholastic Inc., 730 Broadway, New York, NY 10003, by arrangement with Crabtree Publishing Company.
Printed in the U.S.A.
ISBN 0-590-46455-8

3 4 5 6 7 8 9 10   08   99 98 97 96 95 94

these people live. People create communities because they need one another. Places become communities when the people who live in an area share food, work, buildings, and laws. When this happens, a community or village is born!

A living museum

When you visit a museum, you see many things from the past. Historic villages are like living museums. They allow you to experience what life was like in an earlier time. By exploring an historic village, you will feel as if you have walked through a time machine. You will learn about the people who settled the country by observing them in action.

Guides at historic villages wear costumes and pretend to be settlers who lived many years ago. They carry out the daily tasks and jobs that the settlers once performed.

(opposite) The Native People of North America (bottom, right) lived on the land without building towns. Settlers such as the Mennonites (bottom, left) came to this land to practice their religion. The settlers sometimes traveled to their plots of land in wagons pulled by oxen (top).

(below) Settlers traveled long distances by ship, canoe, and wagon. During your visit to a village from the past, find out when people first settled there. From which countries did they come? What were their reasons for leaving their old homes? Why did they choose this place as their new home? What language or languages did they speak? What were their religious beliefs?

Who were the settlers?

Most of you know that the settlers lived in the past. They sailed to North America from France, England, Scotland, Italy, Germany, and other countries in Europe. The earliest settlers, who made their homes in the wilderness, were known as **pioneers**. Later, some settlers moved from one part of the continent to another. Some went west to find new homes; others traveled north. All these people were called **settlers** because they changed, or "settled," the land.

Non-native people

When we talk about pioneers and settlers, we must remember that both these words refer to non-native people. The settlers were newcomers, whereas the Native People of North America have lived here for thousands of years. Unlike the settlers, however, they did not change the land by building towns. They believed that the land was for everyone to use. The settlers, on the other hand, thought it was right to "own" and change the land.

Why did people become settlers?

People left their homes in Europe for many reasons. Some were not allowed to practice their religions in their home countries. Others did not like the way their countries were ruled. Those who were poor wanted to have better lives. Wars also caused people to leave their homelands. The settlers all had one common goal—richer, happier, brighter futures!

Working together

When the first settlers arrived, many hardships awaited them. They were alone in the wilderness. There were no houses, roads, stores, or restaurants. They had to find food and build shelter without any help. It took every ounce of strength to stay alive.

Good neighbors

The settlers who moved into areas where other people lived were much more fortunate. Families who already had homes helped new settlers build houses and barns. The earlier settlers remembered the hard time they had had when they first arrived, so they were happy to help out.

All the members of a community got together to erect buildings such as barns, mills, churches, and schoolhouses. These friendly gatherings were called building bees.

8

Whenever a building such as a mill or school needed to be built, the whole community became involved.

A growing community

After the settlers built shelters, they started growing crops and raising animals. Many of them, however, had not been farmers in their former homes. Some were craftspeople, and others were professionals such as doctors and lawyers. As a community started to form, these skilled settlers began doing other jobs as well as farming. They made objects called **goods**, which they sold or traded with the other settlers. The settlers who were professionals offered special help, called **services**, to others.

Settlers of all ages had to possess a whole variety of skills. The boy above is learning how to handle farm animals. Here are just a few of the things you would have had to learn how to do if you were a settler:
- *milk a cow*
- *chop down trees*
- *build a home from logs*
- *plant and harvest crops*
- *raise farm animals*
- *hunt, trap, and fish*
- *spin wool and weave cloth*
- *make shoes and clothes*
- *bake bread and make butter*
- *make soap and candles*

Map of a village

If you walk down the streets of the historic village you are visiting, you will likely pass a river, pond, or lake. The settlers chose to live in areas near water because they needed it for drinking, cooking, and washing.

The settlers also used the power of water to perform some of their hardest tasks. Two of these tasks were grinding grain and making planks from logs. When a village provided people with these two services, life became a lot less difficult.

Look at the map of this historic village. Find the gristmill, general store, blacksmith shop, barrel maker, wagon maker, church, and school. Which settlers provided goods to the community? Which provided services? In your opinion, which service was the most important? Why? If you were to build your own village, what goods and services would you provide?

The gristmill

The settlers relied on bread to provide them with nutrition. Bread was their **staple**, or the food they ate every day. Bread is made from flour, which comes from plants such as wheat, corn, rye, and oats. The grains of these plants are very hard and must be pounded or ground up to make flour.

A gristmill was usually two or three stories high, which made it the largest building in a new village. As soon as it was built, more settlers moved to the area.

At first, the settlers ground their grain by hand. It was a very difficult job. As soon as there were enough settlers in an area, a gristmill was built. The gristmill used machinery to grind grain.

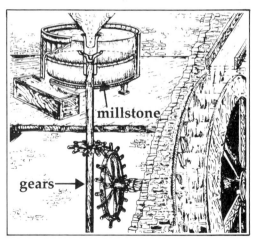

The millpond

The gristmill needed the power of flowing water to grind grain into flour. In order to make sure there was always enough water to operate the mill, the settlers built a dam across a stream or river. The dammed-up water became a millpond. The millpond provided a steady flow of water to the waterwheel, which turned the wheel and ground the grain.

More than just flour

As well as grinding grain, the gristmill made life much less difficult for the settlers in other ways. Farmers could now grow more grain and trade the extra flour for items their families needed. A gristmill also attracted new settlers to the area, causing the village to grow very quickly.

*Water fell into the buckets of the waterwheel and turned this enormous structure. The energy created by the turning waterwheel was carried to the millstones by a set of wheels called **gears**. The gears turned the millstone, which ground grain into flour. The miller, above, holds two pails. One contains grain, one flour.*

The sawmill

Before the sawmill, settlers used **whipsaws** *to cut logs into planks. One person stood on a platform above the log; the other stood below. It took a long time to saw a single plank, and the settlers needed thousands.*

Surrounded by trees, the settlers lived in a world of wood. They made their homes, furniture, and many of their tools from wood. People ate off wooden plates. Food was stored in wooden bins, barrels, and buckets. Children played with wooden toys, and people traveled in wooden carriages that had wooden wheels. In the days of the settlers, there were no factories to produce steel, glass, or plastic, so wood was used to make almost everything.

Using the power of water

In order to get wood, the settlers had to chop down trees and then cut the logs into smaller pieces with hand saws. This was hard work that took a long time. The settlers built sawmills to do this work for them. The sawmill used the energy that water provided, just as the gristmill did. A waterwheel turned, creating the power to saw logs into planks.

The need for planks

The sawmill cut heavy logs into light, even planks that were easy to use. Planks were needed to build homes, barns, and fences. The early log cabins put up by the settlers had only one room and a dirt floor. Using planks, settlers could build two-story houses that had many rooms and wooden floors.

As soon as a sawmill was built, woodworkers opened shop. The sawmill cut heavy logs into planks that were used to build houses and make furniture.

The general store was a welcome resting spot for the farmers who traveled great distances to have their grain ground at the gristmill. This popular meeting place served as the post office, as well. People who lived nearby came once a week to pick up their mail.

16

The general store

T he people in early villages used very little money. They traded goods and services for other goods and services. If they had extra grain, they exchanged it for planks from the sawmill or eggs from another farm. People who were skilled in making things traded the products they made for goods and services offered by others. This type of trading was called the **barter system**.

The trading center

The general store became the trading center in the community. The storekeeper recorded the debts owed and the trades made. These records were like bank accounts. The farmers brought the extra crops they grew to the store. In exchange, they took away goods of their choice. As well as products made by villagers, the general store carried items that came from faraway places.

A meeting place

The general store was not just a trading center. It was also the meeting place in the village. In summer, people relaxed on the front porch. In winter, they sat around the stove discussing community events or playing checkers.

Use your senses!

A visit to the general store is a sensational experience. A general store is full of wonderful things to do, see, taste, and smell. Look at all the gadgets displayed on the shelves. Smell the spices in the spice bins. Taste some licorice or saltwater taffy. Make a list of all the things in the store that appealed to your senses.

Settlers spent most of their time in the kitchen because it was the warmest place in the house. As well as heating the home, the fireplace was used for light, cooking, and baking.

(inset) The early settler homes were made from logs. After a sawmill was built near the village, the settlers were able to build bigger and better houses from planks of wood.

(opposite) The settler child who had his or her own bedroom was very lucky. This child's father even made a rocking horse!

A settler home

Now it is time to visit a settler home in the village. Have you noticed that many of the things that you have in your home are missing from the settler home? Electric lights, modern appliances, and bathrooms are just some of the things that make your life much more comfortable than the lives of the settlers.

Everything the settlers needed was made in the home. The settler shown above is making candles.

Drinking tea and entertaining friends were activities reserved for the parlor (right).

The woodworkers

Every early community needed people who were good at working with wood because wood was the main **raw material** available to the settlers. The woodworkers in the village provided both goods and services.

Carpenters

Carpenters used wood for building. They put up houses and made tables, chairs, and cabinets. They knew every type of wood. They could tell which wood was strong and which would bend easily. They were also skilled in cutting wood in just the right way so it would fit together properly, look its best, and last a long time.

Coopers made barrels

Coopers made buckets, barrels, and tubs. Since there was no metal, plastic, or rubber in the early days, these wooden containers were used to store almost everything. Eggs were placed in barrels filled with sawdust. Liquids were also kept in barrels. The community needed hundreds of barrels, so the cooper was always busy.

*The barrelmaker was called a **cooper**. The cooper bound planks called **staves** together with wooden or metal hoops, as shown above. He heated the barrel over a small stove to make the staves bend more easily.*

In the early days, when nails were hard to get, carpenters were able to build things using wooden pegs.

In some villages, carpenters built homes and made furniture. In this village, a cabinet maker made the furniture.

The cooper bought planks of wood from the sawmill and shaped them perfectly to make sure his containers did not leak. He made the tops and bottoms of the planks narrower than the middle section. Why do you think he did this? If you look at the shape of a barrel, you will see why.

Wheelwrights *made wheels, and* **wainwrights** *made wagons. These artisans were in great demand in the early community. Farmers needed wagons for travel and for transporting goods from one place to another. Both wagons and wheels were mostly wood and needed constant repairs because the roads were bumpy and rough.*

21

PLOW
POINTS
SOLD HERE

The metalworkers

anvil

The blacksmith worked at a raised brick hearth called a **forge***. Giant* **bellows** *fanned the fire. The blacksmith could change the shape of hot iron by hammering it on a workbench called an* **anvil***. He used hammers of various shapes and sizes.*

T he blacksmith was usually the first metalworker to open shop in the village. He worked mostly with iron, which is black. That is why he was called a "blacksmith."

The blacksmith created fireplace tools and cooking utensils for the home. He made hoops for the cooper's barrels and wheel coverings for the wheelwright. Carpenters relied on him for nails, latches, and hinges, and farmers needed him to make farming implements. Some blacksmiths made horseshoes for oxen and horses and nailed them onto the hoofs of the animals, although this job was usually done by a special metalworker called a **farrier**.

Pewter, silver, and tin

The pewterer and silversmith created objects for the home and for other artisans. These metalworkers poured hot, melted metal into molds in order to form the shapes of the objects they wanted to make. Shoe buckles, buttons, candlesticks, dishes, spoons, cups, and teapots are some examples of their creations.

Tin is a soft, silvery-white metal. It was used to make all kinds of things such as pails, lanterns, and kitchen utensils. The tinsmith hammered sheets of metal into these useful objects. The tinsmith was also known as the whitesmith. Can you guess why?

When people started using stoves instead of fireplaces, they needed lighter pots. The tinsmith also created many other useful items for the home. Name five objects the tinsmith made.

Perhaps your class has taken part in a "settler school day." Did your teacher use a school bell? Did you have to sit up straight and recite arithmetic drills? Did you have a spelling bee? Was anyone told to stand in the corner wearing a "dunce" cap? What recess games did you play? How is a settler school day similar to a day at your school? How is it different?

The one-room school

Imagine being a child in the days of the settlers. You would have spent most of your day helping your parents with the chores around the farm, mill, or general store. There would have been very little time left for playing with your friends. You may not have had any friends at all because your neighbors lived so far away!

Building a schoolhouse

As the community grew, so did the number of children. Soon it was time for the settlers to build a school. The schoolhouse they built was very plain. It was one big room filled with rows of desks and benches. Children of all ages were taught in the same class.

The teacher

The teacher was a respected person in the community. He or she provided the settlers with an extremely important service—educating their children. Together the villagers had to pay his or her wages. Some of them offered the teacher meals and a place to sleep. Others provided clothing or school supplies.

Children learned reading, writing, and arithmetic from one teacher. There were very few school supplies such as books or maps. Paper was expensive and hard to get. Instead, children wrote on slates with slate pencils (below). Similar to black-boards, slates could be rubbed clean.

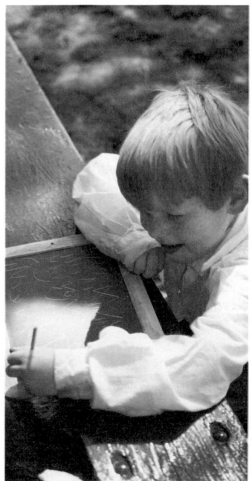

How did they?

How was sickness treated?

The settlers had home remedies for curing simple ailments such as headaches or stomachaches, but there were no treatments for illnesses such as diabetes. Many people, especially children, died from diseases that are easily cured today. Doctors were taught how to deliver babies and amputate, or cut off, arms and legs. One of the most popular cures in those days was **bloodletting.** This treatment was supposed to get rid of "bad blood," which was thought to cause disease.

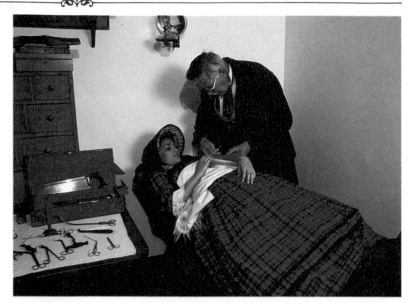

How did settlers travel?

Traveling from place to place was difficult. The few roads that existed were either mud roads or corduroy roads, which were bumpy because they were made of logs. Travel by boat was easier, but not everyone lived near a river or lake. In winter, sleighs pulled by horses glided easily over snow and ice, making travel much less difficult. During the rest of the year, the settlers used wagons, carriages, boats, and their own legs to get from place to place.

Did the settlers have jobs?

Most of the settlers were farmers. The miller, sawyer, storekeeper, and schoolteacher all performed important jobs, too. Young people sometimes worked as **apprentices** to crafts-people. Many men were loggers in the wintertime. Women took extra jobs cooking, baking, or doing laundry for others.

How did they get news?

In early villages, people told one another the news at the gristmill or the general store. News from other places came to the village by mail or was told to the storekeeper by the stagecoach driver. In the bigger villages, printers opened shop and started newspapers.

Did they go to church?

The early villages often did not have a church, so the villagers assembled to worship at their homes, the schoolhouse, or the general store. When many people of the same faith moved to a community, they usually built a church. The priests or ministers traveled from community to community. They were known as **circuit preachers** because they made a full circuit, or circle, in their travels.

Children had very few playthings. Sometimes their fathers carved toys from wood or their mother made them cornhusk dolls or apple dolls.

(opposite, top) The settlers are at a corn husking. They always tried to make work fun by doing it together. Harvest was another time of celebration (opposite, bottom). Once the crops were in and the hard work finished, it was time for fun!

On Sundays, children were expected to take part in religious activities. The Noah's Ark was the only toy they could play with on this day.

Settler fun

The settlers found many ways to have fun even while they worked. They held work parties called bees in order to get difficult jobs done. At a bee, people of the community came together to help one another complete a task that required many hands. There were barn-raising bees, building bees, corn-husking bees, quilting bees, apple bees, and taffy-pulling bees. The host supplied a hearty meal as payment for the help. The settlers ate and danced after the work was finished.

Holidays

Although the first settlers did not have much time to celebrate holidays, the later ones looked forward to these special times. Christmas was the biggest holiday of the year. The settlers went to church and enjoyed the company of their friends and neighbors. Other holidays celebrated by the settlers were Valentine's Day, Thanksgiving, and Easter. These special days were set aside for family and friends.

Simple pleasures for children

Both parents and children had fun at outings and events such as fall and winter fairs. Children also enjoyed playing with other children. They skipped rope, chased hoops, and played tag.

What was your experience?

As a guide to an historic village, this woman helps children learn about the past. What interesting things did your guide teach you?

Now that you have visited a village from the past, either with your school or in this book, do you think you would have enjoyed living in settler times? What would have been the most fun about living in those days? What would you not have enjoyed? Which toys or appliances would you have missed the most from your way of life today? If you visited a village, what did you learn that you could not learn from a book? What did you learn from this book that you did not learn at the village? Why are both ways of learning important? Can you remember the things you learned on other travels or field trips? Which trip has taught you the most? Why?

Glossary

apprentice - A person who learns a skill by working for a craftsperson

artisan - A skilled craftsperson

barter system - A system of trading goods and services without using money

community - A group of people who live together in one area and share buildings, services, and a way of life. A community is also the place in which these people live.

cooper - A craftsperson who makes barrels, buckets, and tubs

corduroy road - A road made of logs

dam - A wall built across a river or stream to stop the flow of water

debt - Money, goods, or services that someone owes someone else

early settler - A person who is among the first people to settle in an area. A settler from an early time in history. A pioneer

farrier - A craftsperson who shoes horses

gear - A wheel with teeth around its edge that meshes with the teeth of another wheel. Gears transfer power from one part of a machine to another.

general store - The main store in a settler community. It carries many kinds of supplies for trade or sale.

goods - Items that are made to be sold

gristmill - A mill that grinds grain

historic - Important in history. Historic places are important because they teach us how the people who settled this continent lived in the past.

lantern - A type of candle or lamp that has a protective case

millstones - A pair of large stones used for grinding grain in a gristmill

Native People - A group of people who were born in an area and whose ancestors were the first to live in that region

parlor - A special room in which guests are entertained

pewterer - A craftsperson who molds objects from pewter, which is made from tin and lead

pioneer - One of the first people to settle in an area

plank - A long, thick board that has been sawed from a log

product - Something made as a result of work and skill

professional - A person who makes a living performing a highly skilled type of work

raw material - A material such as wood or iron from which products are made

sawmill - A mill that saws planks of wood

sawyer - A person who operates a sawmill

service - Work done for others that does not produce goods

settler - A person who makes his or her home in a new country or part of a country that is not built up

silversmith - A person who makes things out of silver

staple - A basic food that is eaten every day, such as rice or bread

wilderness - A place or region that has not been changed by people

woodworker - A craftsperson who works with wood

Index

Acknowledgments

Cover photograph:
Metro Region Conservation Authority.

Title page photograph:
Metro Region Conservation Authority.

At Black Creek Pioneer Village:
Marc Crabtree: p.13(left), 19(bottom), 21(middle);
Metro Region Conservation Authority: p.4, 5(top and bottom), 7(top), 13(right), 18(top), 19(top left and top right), 24, 26(top, bottom), 27(middle and bottom), 28, 29(top and bottom), 30.

At Lang Pioneer Village:
Jim Bryant: p.12.

At Saint-Marie Among the Hurons:
Jim Bryant: p.27(top); Saint-Marie Among the Hurons, Midland: p.7(bottom right), 14.

At Upper Canada Village:
Jim Bryant: p.8, 15(bottom left), 21(top), 23;
Ken Faris: p.9, 15(bottom right), 18(inset).

Other photographs:
Jim Bryant: p.25(left), Bob Mansour: p.6, 7(bottom left), 15(top), 20, 21(bottom), 22, 25(right), 26(middle).

Illustrations:
Cover: John Mantha; Halina Below-Spada: p.13;
National Archives of Canada/C-1115, Un Magasin général de Jadis, Edmond J. Massicotte: p.16-17;
Helen Jean Smith: p.10-11, David Willis: p.14, 28.